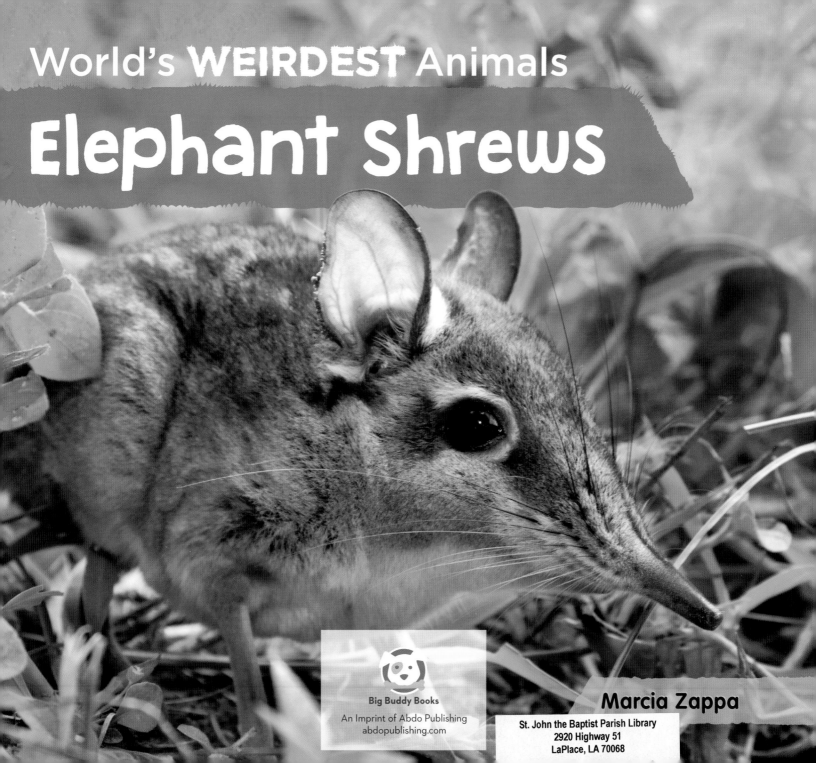

World's **WEIRDEST** Animals

Elephant Shrews

Big Buddy Books

An Imprint of Abdo Publishing
abdopublishing.com

Marcia Zappa

abdopublishing.com

Published by Abdo Publishing, a division of ABDO, PO Box 398166, Minneapolis, Minnesota 55439. Copyright © 2016 by Abdo Consulting Group, Inc. International copyrights reserved in all countries. No part of this book may be reproduced in any form without written permission from the publisher. Big Buddy Books™ is a trademark and logo of Abdo Publishing.

Printed in the United States of America, North Mankato, Minnesota.
042015
092015

Cover Photos: Ivan Kuzmin/Glow Images; Shutterstock.com.
Interior Photos: Heinrich van den Berg/Getty Images (p. 23); EBFoto/Deposit Photos (p. 5); Daniel Heuclin/NPL/
     Minden Pictures (p. 30); ©iStockphoto.com (p. 15); Jabruson/NPL/Minden Pictures (p. 9); Ivan Kuzmin/
     Glow Images (p. 29); Idelfoto/Deposit Photos (p. 17); Mark MacEwen/NPL/Minden Pictures (p. 27); Clyde
     Nishimura, Smithsonian's National Zoo (p. 25); M. Schäf/Glow Images (p. 7); Shutterstock.com (pp. 11, 19);
     Richard du Toit/Getty Images (p. 21).

Coordinating Series Editor: Rochelle Baltzer
Contributing Editors: Tamara L. Britton, Megan M. Gunderson, Bridget O'Brien, Sarah Tieck
Graphic Design: Adam Craven

Library of Congress Cataloging-in-Publication Data

Zappa, Marcia, 1985- author.
  Elephant shrews / Marcia Zappa.
      pages cm. -- (World's weirdest animals)
  ISBN 978-1-62403-774-0
  1. Elephant shrews--Juvenile literature. I. Title.
  QL444.M242Z37 2016
  599.33'7--dc23
                    2015004767

Contents

Wildly Weird!

The world is full of weird, wonderful animals. Elephant shrews, or *sengis* (SEHN-gees), live in Africa. There are almost 20 types of elephant shrews.

These small animals are known for their long, movable snouts. Most elephant shrews choose one mate for life. And, they keep a set of clear trails so they can quickly escape predators. These unusual features make elephant shrews wildly weird!

Elephant shrews look like other shrews. But, they are not related. In fact, elephant shrews are more closely related to elephants!

Bold Bodies

Elephant shrews are **mammals**. Their bodies are covered in soft, thick fur. The fur can be black, brown, gray, gold, white, or tan.

An elephant shrew has a small, rounded body. Its long, thin tail is slightly shorter than its body. An elephant shrew has short front legs and long back legs. Its head features large eyes and ears.

BODY

EAR

EYE

SNOUT

TAIL

LEG

TOES

7

Different types of elephant shrews vary in size. Adults weigh 1 to 25 ounces (30 to 700 g). They grow 3.5 to 12 inches (9 to 31 cm) long.

The short-eared elephant shrew is the smallest type of elephant shrew. The giant elephant shrew (*below*) is the largest.

9

Super Snouts

Elephant shrews are named for their long, movable **snouts**. The snout is similar to an elephant's trunk. At the end are an elephant shrew's **nostrils**. The shrew twists and turns its snout to move away leaves while searching for food.

Elephant shrews use their strong sense of smell to find food. They also have good hearing and sight.

11

Where in the World?

Elephant shrews live in southern, eastern, and northwestern Africa. They live in different habitats. These include grasslands, woodlands, and forests. Elephant shrews are also found in dry, open areas and jungles.

Did You Know?

Elephant shrews often choose habitats that can hide them from predators.

Europe

Asia

Africa

Australia

Pacific
Ocean

Atlantic
Ocean

Indian Ocean

N
W E
S

= Elephant Shrew Region

Home Sweet Home

Elephant shrews have different types of homes. Some build nests on the forest floor. These are usually made of dry leaves.

Others rest under fallen trees or thick bushes. Some live in cracks in rocks or holes in the ground. Some dig **burrows** or use burrows left behind by other animals.

Most elephant shrews are active during the day. They rest in their homes at night.

A Shrew's Life

Most elephant shrews choose one **mate** for life. A male and female pair come together four to five times a year to **breed**. The rest of the time, they live separate lives.

When not together, elephant shrew mates use scent to keep track of each other.

An elephant shrew pair lives in the same home area. The home area often includes several acres of land.

An elephant shrew pair does not allow others to enter their home area. Males guard their territory from other males. Females guard it from other females.

Elephant shrews keep away strangers by screaming, snapping, and kicking.

Escape Plan

Elephant shrews have many **predators**. These include snakes, lizards, and large birds such as raptors.

Many elephant shrews make trails through their home areas. They check them often and keep them clear. When faced with a predator, an elephant shrew runs away on one of its trails.

Did You Know?

Elephant shrews run on their toes. Some types can run about 18 miles (29 km) an hour!

An elephant shrew's long back legs make it good at jumping. This helps it escape predators.

Favorite Foods

Elephant shrews are omnivores (AHM-nih-vawrs). That means they eat both plants and animals. They eat seeds, berries, green plants, worms, and spiders. They often eat insects. This includes ants, termites, and beetles.

Elephant shrews eat during the day.
This is unusual for small mammals.

Life Cycle

Female elephant shrews give birth to one or two babies at a time. A mother elephant shrew must leave her newborn to search for food. She leaves her baby in a well-hidden spot. She returns several times a day so her baby can drink her milk and grow.

When elephant shrew babies are born, they are already covered in fur.

When it is two to three weeks old, a young elephant shrew begins following its mother around. It learns how to **survive** by watching her. After one to two months, it is ready to live on its own.

In time, elephant shrews leave their parents' home areas. They set off to find mates and make their own home areas.

World Wide Weird

Most types of elephant shrews are common. But a few types are at risk. Roads, farms, and buildings have split up their forest habitat. This can make it difficult for them to find food and mates.

It is important to know how our actions affect wild animals. With care, we can keep weird, wonderful animals such as elephant shrews around for years to come.

Elephant shrews live up to five years in the wild.

FAST FACTS ABOUT:
Elephant Shrews

Animal Type – mammal

Size – 3.5 to 12 inches (9 to 31 cm) long

Weight – 1 to 25 ounces (30 to 700 g)

Habitat – grasslands, woodlands, forests, dry open areas, and jungles in Africa

Diet – ants, termites, beetles, worms, spiders, seeds, berries, and green plants

What makes the elephant shrew wildly weird?

It has a long, moveable snout, it keeps a set of trails for escaping predators, and it usually chooses one mate for life.

Glossary

breed to produce animals by mating.

burrow an animal's underground home.

habitat a place where a living thing is naturally found.

mammal a member of a group of living beings. Mammals make milk to feed their babies and usually have hair or fur on their skin.

mate a partner to join with in order to reproduce, or have babies.

nostril an opening of a nose.

predator a person or animal that hunts and kills animals for food.

snout a part of the face, including the nose and the mouth, that sticks out. Some animals, such as elephant shrews, have a snout.

survive to continue to live or exist.

Websites

To learn more about World's Weirdest Animals, visit **booklinks.abdopublishing.com**. These links are routinely monitored and updated to provide the most current information available.

Index